CAREER

COMPASS

CAREER C⊘MPASS

A guided journal for discovering a fulfilling
career path and designing a life you love

BY DR. COLLEEN CAMPBELL

CHRONICLE BOOKS

SAN FRANCISCO

ISBN 978-1-7972-0185-6

Manufactured in India.

MIX
Paper from
responsible sources
FSC™ C010615
www.fsc.org

Design by Kat Yao.

10 9 8 7 6 5 4 3 2 1

Chronicle books and gifts are available at special quantity discounts to corporations, professional associations, literacy programs, and other organizations. For details and discount information, please contact our premiums department at corporatesales@chroniclebooks.com or at 1-800-759-0190.

Chronicle Books LLC
680 Second Street
San Francisco, California 94107
www.chroniclebooks.com

INTRODUCTION

> The most difficult thing is the decision to act. The rest is merely tenacity. The fears are paper tigers. You can do anything you decide to do. You can act to change and control your life and the procedure. The process is its own reward.
>
> —AMELIA EARHART

As a kid, I remember hearing, "You're not supposed to like your job. It's just what you do to make money." I didn't believe that then, and I certainly don't believe that now. You can (and should) find a career path that's aligned with who you are. You can absolutely be engaged and energized by your work, and you can develop yourself professionally in ways that are satisfying and fulfilling. Let this journal be your guide.

As a psychologist, my area of expertise is how people change, how to support that change, and what can get in the way. I bring this perspective to my work as an executive coach and career coach. After years of working with clients in all areas and at all levels—from tech, business, and the legal field to the arts, entertainment, non-profits, and more—I've come to the conclusion that achieving career success is a holistic pursuit. It involves self-awareness, self-work, and strategy. Once you know who you are at work, you can begin to understand your full potential, as well as your blind spots and weaknesses. While success means different things to different people, the universal factor is engagement. This journal will take you through a process of self-discovery that will empower you to attain consistent engagement and career fulfillment.

When our career-coaching clients walk through our doors, it's because they want to make improvements or changes in their careers, whether the focus is on professional development in their current role or mapping out a next step that's the right fit. Whatever the reason, in almost all cases, we begin our work together by assessing and discussing their personality, strengths, and values. Note that personality and strengths are neurological: They reflect how we are wired. And while these things can evolve (since our brains are constantly learning and growing), often these aspects of who we are remain fairly constant. Therefore, reflecting on our core personality offers a wealth of information about what works for us, what doesn't, and the best strategies for our success.

This journal will be very similar to working with your own career coach. We will start with questions and prompts meant to inventory who you are—your personality, strengths, and values—and how that relates to your career, both on a high level and on a day-to-day level. Then, we will map out your requirements for work and create a list of things that need to be in place for you to thrive. We call this list your Career Criteria. From there, we will use your Career Criteria to determine your customized career goals and brainstorm potential paths. Once we've identified a clear path, what we'll call your Career North Star, we will create a concrete action plan to break into that industry or land that dream job. Finally, to round it all out, there are some essential career tips and useful job search strategies to help you on your way.

Before we get started, here are a few guidelines to help you answer the questions to the best of your ability.

1 If you are just graduating or work in a field that is not a fit for you, answer these questions by reflecting on your experiences in school or in other parts of your life where you feel you've been thriving. Then consider how this might relate to work life. Try to connect the dots or look for parallels.

2 As we age, we can become more flexible in our personality and strengths. If at any point you are struggling to answer a question or you feel like you can relate to both sides of a prompt, think back to what you were like when you were younger. This can help reveal your core patterns and inclinations, the ones that are neurologically hardwired. Catalog how and why you may have changed and what that might mean for your career.

3 Another useful strategy is to consider questions in terms of your preference. In other words, you can adapt (to varying degrees) to different circumstances, but what would you choose if you could pick any way of being or working? For example, a person could act more extroverted at work because that's what helps them achieve their goals, when they are actually more of an introvert. Thinking in terms of how you act and behave when you're most relaxed and feel most like yourself is one way to figure out your preference.

Your preference reveals what comes easiest to you, those skills that come from the dominant areas of your brain. You want a large portion of what you do in your career to be in this sweet spot. Can you stretch from there? Of course! I hope you do! But you need a balance between growing and pushing yourself and operating from this sweet spot. You will have the most success when your work is aligned with who you are naturally. So, as you reflect on the following questions, base your answers not on the roles you play at work or home, or what your current circumstances are, but rather on what your deepest preferences are—what you choose to do when nothing is on the line.

4 This journal is primarily for recent graduates and those early in their career, but it will also be useful for those who are deeper into their career path. For this latter group, the journal can help you pivot into a different area or make small changes so your career path becomes a better fit day to day.

NOW, LET'S DIVE IN.

Identifying Your Career Personality

This section focuses on assessing and observing your personality, strengths, and values, and how they resonate with different industries, work cultures, leadership styles, roles, and responsibilities.

Have you ever had a friend enthusiastically recommend a book to you that you just weren't able to get into? Perhaps the topic didn't interest you, or the writing style didn't capture your attention. In the same vein, there are career areas that you won't do as well in because they aren't aligned with your aptitude, interests, or the way your mind works. The following questions will allow you to reflect on who you are and how this aligns (or doesn't align) with different types of careers.

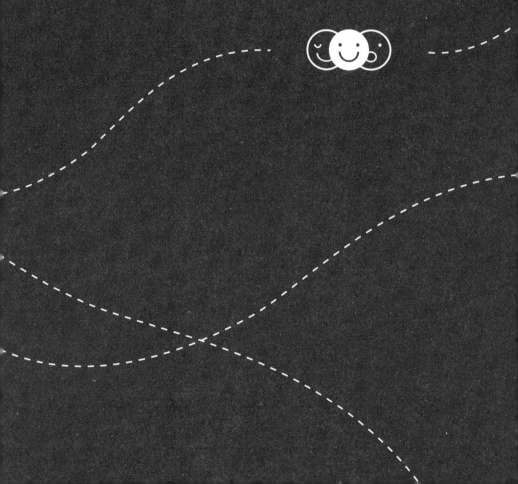

Are you **EXTROVERTED** or **INTROVERTED**?

Are you energized by being with others?	Do you recharge by spending time alone and need time to reflect on and digest your day?
Do you prefer to express yourself without filtering your thoughts, i.e., "thinking out loud"?	Do you like to consider your thoughts before expressing them?
Do you get a burst of energy by initiating action or taking charge of a situation?	Do you tend to think things through before making a decision or moving forward?
Do you feel open to answering questions about yourself?	Do you have a sense of privacy about certain topics and personal information?
Do you learn best by doing?	Do you learn best by reflection and mental practice?
IF YOU ANSWERED MOSTLY YES, YOU'RE MORE **EXTROVERTED**	IF YOU ANSWERED MOSTLY YES, YOU'RE MORE **INTROVERTED**

Note the ways you identify as an extrovert or an introvert, and remember, it's not all black and white. In fact, you may fall right in the middle. That's fine. Jot down some thoughts about what this might mean in terms of your day-to-day environment and role.

What percentage of time in your workday do you like to be with people versus working alone? Think of times you've participated in group projects that required a lot of collaboration as well as instances when you've worked on your own. When were you more productive? More creative? Happier?

Do you like to shoot from the hip at meetings or do you prefer some time to think over what you're going to share? What does that say about the kind of environment or work culture you might opt for?

Are you a CONCRETE or ABSTRACT thinker?

Do you prefer to focus on information that is concrete and practical, "here and now"?	Do you like to take in information that is abstract, big picture, and future oriented?
Do you like to come to a conclusion by collecting all the facts to thoroughly support your perspective?	Do you often notice patterns in the world around you and draw conclusions from those patterns?
If someone gave you a single-page project overview and asked for feedback, would you ask follow-up questions in order to be careful and in-depth with your conclusion?	If someone gave you a single-page project overview and asked for feedback, would you get the gist of the project and then give a high-level, brush-stroke perspective?
Do you tend to remember specific details and facts (that is, things we know for sure)?	Do you like theories and ideas, and value imagination and innovation?
If you had to teach a class, would you enjoy teaching a fact-based class, like history or chemistry?	If you had to teach a class, would you enjoy teaching a theoretical class, like philosophy, sociology, or a seminar on feminism?
IF YOU ANSWERED MOSTLY YES, THEN YOU'RE MORE OF A **CONCRETE THINKER**	IF YOU ANSWERED MOSTLY YES, THEN YOU'RE MORE OF AN **ABSTRACT THINKER**

Oftentimes, people who are more concrete prefer work that is tangible in nature. At the end of the day, they are most satisfied when they can see what they've accomplished. They are present-tense oriented, meaning their focus is on the here and now. So, they feel satisfied in careers where everything is happening in the present, like nursing, accounting, law enforcement, cooking, or teaching elementary school.

People who are more abstract like to focus on possibilities, innovation, strategic initiatives, ideas, and change creation. They might prefer a career as a social worker, software developer, philosopher, product designer, research scientist, or strategic planner.

What do you think having more concrete or abstract tendencies might say about the kind of work you prefer?

It can be stressful, disengaging, or boring for someone who is more concrete to be in an abstract work environment, and vice versa. When have you found a subject stressful, dull, or hard to focus on? What does that tell you about your tendencies toward the concrete or abstract?

When do you tend to be most energized, inspired, or engaged at work or in your studies? What are you doing during these times? Are you with people? Are you focused on concrete or abstract information?

Decision-making: RATIONAL or RELATIONAL?

Do you tend to make logical decisions, setting aside your emotions in order to be as objective as possible?

Do you tend to make decisions that are values based and people oriented, "feeling out" the best decision?

Do you consider yourself analytical and enjoy critiquing?

Do you consider yourself naturally empathetic and compassionate, and prefer harmony over productive conflict and debate?

Do you value efficiency and truth, even over diplomacy?

Are you good at reading body language?

IF YOU ANSWERED MOSTLY YES, YOU TEND TO BE MORE

RATIONAL

IF YOU ANSWERED MOSTLY YES, YOU TEND TO BE MORE

RELATIONAL

People who lean toward rational decision-making often do well in career paths related to rational systems, such as computer science, architecture, mathematics, law, life sciences, or data science. Whereas value-based decision-makers do well in career paths that are more people oriented, like teaching, sales, human services (like social work and psychotherapy), or hospitality. For those types of roles, it's important to have naturally high emotional intelligence and find solving people's problems engaging, rather than frustrating or tedious.

Now that you've identified the type of decision-maker you are, what do you think that says about your potential career path? If you are already well into your career, does this shine light on why aspects of your career may or may not suit you?

Are you **STRUCTURED** or **FLEXIBLE?**

STRUCTURE	FLEXIBILITY
Do you like to work in a well-thought-out, organized way?	Do you prefer to live in an uninhibited, flexible, casual way?
Are you routine oriented?	Are you able to easily adapt to changing circumstances?
Do you find it energizing to check things off your list?	Do you need variety to stay engaged?
Do you prefer not to bend rules?	When you get into a flow with something do you tend to lose track of time?
Do you like to get things done and feel in control?	Do you like to work against the pressure of a deadline, even up to the last minute?
IF YOU ANSWERED MOSTLY YES, YOU PREFER **STRUCTURE**	IF YOU ANSWERED MOSTLY YES, YOU PREFER **FLEXIBILITY**

Generally speaking, routine-oriented, methodical people will perform better in organized, well-functioning environments with good systems in place; whereas, those on the more spontaneous side need variety, new problems to deal with, and situations to adapt to in order to feel fully engaged. What do you think your tendency to be more organized or more flexible might say about the career path that fits you best? What do you think it says about the kind of day-to-day environment that suits you best?

Your *values* are your principles, or what you think is important in life. They (should) determine your priorities, and, deep down, they're probably the measure you use to tell if your life is turning out the way you want it to.

When you're living out your life and career in a way that matches your values, there's a sense of balance, an alignment. When your behaviors and focus are not in accord with your values, there can be burnout, internal conflict, and frustration. That is why making a conscious effort to identify your values is so important.

Identify a time at work (or at school, or even in your personal life) when you felt most at peace, connected, or fulfilled. What do you think this might say about what you value?

Identify a time at work when you felt most energized and alive. What does this reveal about your values?

When do you feel most proud, self-respecting, or satisfied at school or at work? What is happening during those times? What is the focus? Are you solving problems? If yes, what type?

Circle the 3 attributes you value the most in the people you work and spend time with:

IMAGINATIVE

STEADY

DEPENDABLE

INGENIOUS

LOGISTICAL

TACTICAL

OPTIMISTIC

SENSITIVE

INDEPENDENT

FACTUAL

CURIOUS

INTUITIVE

AUTHENTIC

PRAGMATIC

DIPLOMATIC

LOGICAL

ADAPTABLE

PERSUASIVE

PLAYFUL

DETAILED

DARING

CAUTIOUS

CREATIVE

What do you think the words you circled say about what might or might not fit into your career path?

Brainstorm and make a list of your top 10 core values. They may be anything from altruism to consistency to freedom, status, or love. They do not necessarily need to be related to your career—it's just the 10 things you value most and aspire to embody.

As you work through your list, you may find that some values naturally combine. For instance, if you value philanthropy, community, and generosity, you might say that service to others is one of your top values. It is fine to group some of these into "families" and put them on a single line. In other words, it's OK if a family of values takes the space of a single value on the list.

CORE VALUES:

1.	6.
2.	7.
3.	8.
4.	9.
5.	10.

Does your list of values provide insight into what might engage you in a career? Or, what aspect of your current career is most engaging, and what areas are not? What about the type of people you prefer to be around, or the type of work you might find most fulfilling?

Strengths are natural proficiencies and talents. They are the areas where you have the greatest potential for building skill. Developing your strengths is often a better use of time and energy than trying to improve your weaknesses. But being aware of your weaknesses is powerful because you will know what to outsource.

Another key piece of information: you need to actually *use* your strengths in order to thrive. So, if you realize your work doesn't capitalize on your key strengths, that's a problem that needs to be solved immediately.

Create a list of skills, aptitudes, offerings, and talents that we have not yet covered. Include "soft skills" (interpersonal skills) because they are often a blend of several strengths and essential in many work environments.

What strengths and skills have others noticed in you? How about skills you've cultivated in previous jobs, volunteer positions, or school projects?

As a prompt to motivate you, make a list of 4 or 5 times you successfully accomplished something, had a win, or dominated a challenge or problem. (Later you can develop these into narratives or stories to tell in interviews.)

Keep in mind that facets of your personality and strengths can also have a downside. When we're good at something, we tend to utilize that skill even when it's no longer working for us. For example, if you're analytical, that's fantastic. It means you're good at digging to the bottom of something and looking for proof, but the downside is that sometimes you might get caught in analysis paralysis, spinning your wheels indefinitely. Take some time and think about your top strengths and personality assets, and then list what the downside might be for each. To be clear, the benefit of doing this is that you can then watch for those potential pitfalls and switch gears when you begin to fall into that pattern.

Self-awareness is essential to your best performance at work, and more importantly, your quality of life as a whole. It's ironic that knowing ourselves can be so elusive, but such is the nature of our brains. So, we have to utilize a variety of methods to really see ourselves and become the most aware and empowered selves we can be. Asking others for their assessment can be very illuminating. It's not for the faint of heart, but the rewards are worth it!

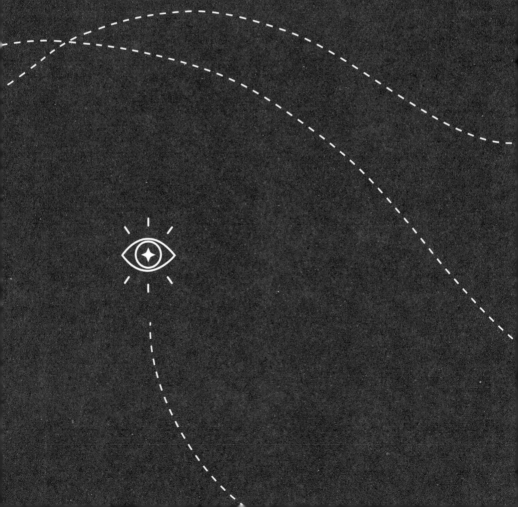

You may have heard of 360-degree reviews, where a certain number of people in your company are asked to give feedback on their experience with you. The following exercise is designed to be your own mini-360 review. Ask a handful of people—family, friends, past colleagues, or teachers—if they can answer the following questions about you as a way to help you learn and grow. Use the following pages to record their answers and any major takeaways.

1

What do you see as my biggest strengths? What about weaknesses?

2

Can you share any feedback about my interpersonal skills?

3

What have you noticed about my problem-solving skills? Can you share any observations?

4

How would you describe my communication skills? Do you think I am good at building rapport with people? How am I as a listener? Do I convey ideas clearly?

5

What do you see as my leadership style, or the characteristics that might inform my leadership style?

6

How do you think I do in the face of change?

7

What do you see as my real talents?

8

Is there any other feedback you would like to give me, or is there something you think I should know?

Developing Your Career Criteria

At this point, you have reflected on your personality character-istics, strengths, and values. Now, we'll use this knowledge to create a list of career requirements, the things that need to be true for you to thrive in a particular role, workplace, or industry. We'll call this list your Career Criteria.

Keep in mind that this is a "living" list, which is to say, you should continue to add to it as you gather more information in the field. As you go through your career search, you can use this as a checklist to filter out any careers that are not a good fit and identify the best path for you.

What do you really love to do? What are your hobbies and interests? How might this translate to your list of career criteria?

For example, if you are obsessed with lifestyle blogs and websites, could that be a clue that you should consider companies in or adjacent to that space? Or perhaps you love sports—why not consider sports journalism, sports broadcasting, sports marketing, team management, coaching, stadium events, or sports law?

List your hobbies and interests here. Could they translate to a career or a side hustle, or should they remain a hobby?

→ This is a useful thought exercise, but it's also important to recognize when a hobby shouldn't necessarily be a career. You should leave no stone unturned, but you also need to be pragmatic about what is a realistic career path, and what should remain a hobby or extracurricular.

Go back to the section on personality traits (pages 12−25), where we went over being extroverted or introverted, concrete or abstract, rational or relational, structured or flexible. Does that section give you ideas about the type of workplace culture that you'd enjoy or the kinds of roles and responsibilities that would fit you best?

....

....

....

....

....

....

....

....

....

....

....

....

....

....

....

....

....

....

....

....

....

Go back to the section on strengths and weaknesses (pages 34–41) and your self-assessment (pages 42–45); what does the information you gathered there say about what you require in a culture, role, or industry in order to thrive?

Do these sections give you ideas for professional development? For example, could it be useful to work on being more organized (or empathetic, or rational) at work? Did you uncover areas of aptitude or skills that you would like to develop? Take notes here on what kinds of professional development might be worth pursuing and how they relate to your requirements in a workplace.

What type of atmosphere, culture, or environment do you prefer at school or at work?

What type of leadership do you respond to? Is mentorship important?

What is your personal definition of success? What needs to be true of a role or company to ensure you can achieve that kind of success?

Reflect on your work history or experience in the classroom and make a list of the aspects that were a fit for you and those that were not, including, but not limited to: type of team; management (or teaching) style; culture; types of colleagues; types of products, projects, or services; and organizational structure.

You make decisions based on your value system and are drawn to people who share those values. Ultimately, they act as a guide in every aspect of your life. For example, if you value health but regularly work 70-hour weeks, how does that make you feel about yourself? And if you don't value competition but work in a highly competitive sales environment, how does this affect your motivation? Flip back to the first chapter and look over the work you did on your values (pages 26–33). How do your values translate into things you need or don't want in a future career path or workplace?

....

....

....

....

....

....

....

....

....

....

....

....

....

....

....

....

....

....

How do your values translate into things you may need or want in your life outside of work, and how might that impact your career path? In other words, is work-life balance important to you? Would you rather work more and earn more, or earn less and have free time for hobbies, side hustles, or family?

If making a meaningful impact on the world around you is a significant piece of your job satisfaction, make a list of the industries, companies, nonprofits, B Corps, and foundations that are meaningful to you. What bigger problems would you like to help solve? Where would you like to make an impact?

How important is an opportunity for advancement to you? Should this be on the requirements list?

How important is learning new things as a regular part of the job? Are perks like ongoing training or a stipend for career coaching valuable to you?

Your career should never be just about the money, but it is still your livelihood. Is there a salary range you're looking for? How important is money? If you're new in the working world, use this space to estimate and calculate your total cost of living. How much is enough? If you're already working and looking to make a change, are you willing to take a cut or is that not an option?

Where do you want to live? Are you willing to move? What kind of lifestyle do you want to have? For example, do you prefer the suburbs or an urban location?

Now take the lists you've made throughout this chapter and compile them into a concise checklist of all your career criteria. This checklist will serve two purposes: vetting your career path ideas to see if they are truly a fit for you and developing questions to ask during interviews.

CAREER CRITERIA:

1.	6.
2.	7.
3.	8.
4.	9.
5.	10.

Now, make a list of 5 things you know you *don't* want in a career or company.

CAREER DEAL BREAKERS:

1.

2.

3.

4.

5.

Looking at your Career Criteria and Career Deal Breakers, consider what questions you could ask a prospective employer to determine if they meet your requirements. Of course, when the time comes, you have to use your best judgment. You obviously want to be sensitive with the questions you ask, and some questions may need to be veiled in some way. However, when you ask questions in the right way, it looks like confidence.

Before you move forward, there's one last thing I want you to do. Look through your condensed checklist and identify your Top 3 Requirements. These are the 3 most important factors, those you will not compromise on. It may be money, work-life balance, location, opportunity for advancement, mission, or something else. List these 3 things here. We'll come back to this later.

TOP 3 REQUIREMENTS:

1

2

3

Brainstorming
Career Paths

Congrats on making it this far in the process! The information you've gathered so far will help you evaluate your options, set goals for professional development, and create long- and short-term action plans.

This section is one big brainstorming exercise to help you generate ideas about potential next steps in your career—whether you're looking for a significant career change, an internal career move, or areas of professional development. This is the place to explore what's possible.

If you're looking for a career change, keep in mind that ideas may come in the form of specific roles or companies, or even a general industry. Some people have a very clear idea of the exact role they want to pursue, whereas others may come to realize their career needs fall into a general arena, like the nonprofit sector, and the exact company or role comes later.

Don't censor too much at this juncture! You can get practical and analytical later, but for now, stay open-minded and allow ideas to flow. Our goal in this section is to generate as many ideas as possible.

Do you have any ideas right off the bat? Are there roles that you've seen or heard about that interest you? Are there certain careers you've dreamed about? Jot these down.

Have people who know you well made career path suggestions to you? Why did they suggest that path? Do any of these resonate enough to go on the list? Write them down here.

Are there people you know—friends, parents, acquaintances—that have careers you admire or envy? What about people you've read about in an article or heard speak on a podcast? Should their career paths be on your list? Jot those ideas down here.

When you were a child, did you have any career fantasies or dreams? When we're young, we play in ways that reveal our core personality, and for some, this might be a clue to a career path. Share these memories here. Then consider if these clues can be connected to a real option today.

Look at your work in the Career Criteria section (pages 74–79), and see if it sparks any ideas. For example, if meaningful work is important to you, begin by asking yourself what is most meaningful to you in all areas of your life. Ask yourself how those things might translate into a career. As another example, if you identified earlier as someone who prefers concrete work and needs to see tangible results in order to feel satisfied, then consider what tangible products interest you. This could be anything from books to electronics to food. These physical products might be a clue to the types of companies you'd want to work at. Brainstorm ideas for each of your Career Criteria here.

Write down all the possible pivot points from where you stand now. A pivot can be thought of in two main ways: 1. Moving to the same position in a completely different industry; or, 2. Staying in the same industry and moving into a different but related role. Pivots tend to be the easiest route to a career change, so this is a useful exercise to understand all your options. Take time to explore and write down the potential options here, even the ones you're not sure about. If you're graduating from school, use this space to brainstorm all the paths you could pursue based on your major or studies. Do these appeal to you? Why or why not?

If you aren't sure what type of role you are interested in, ask yourself if there is an area you want to become an expert in. Is there a skill that you want to master? Are there strengths you want to improve? From there, you can think of pivot points from your current career or studies that might provide those learning experiences. Write your ideas here.

If there's an industry you're interested in, do a survey of all the nearby companies in that space. Try to understand their different functions within the industry so you can identify the companies that are the most interesting to you. Keep track of those companies here.

Research specific companies and careers in your interest areas. You can do general internet searches, such as: companies making a difference in (your area), most innovative companies in (your area), or best roles for creatives. You get the idea. Think about what's important to you and do a search to see if there are articles or lists that give you ideas. Write those ideas here.

Review the *Occupational Outlook Handbook* from the US Bureau of Labor Statistics. Look up your role (or potential role) to learn more about it. Also note what's included in the "Similar Occupations" section. Write your notes here.

Use online databases and networking sites, such as LinkedIn and AngelList, to conduct additional research. Startup databases are built for investors, but can also be used as search engines to better understand a sector of the market or a specific company. LinkedIn is a great tool for researching companies, jobs, and people—look up keywords related to your areas of interest and read through the results for ideas. Write your ideas here.

Reflect on people who have left your current company or role and gone else-where. Look them up on LinkedIn; what are they doing now? If you're graduat-ing, look for alumni from your school and/or people who majored in the same field or studied a similar subject. Where do they work now? What has their path looked like?

Identifying a Career North Star

At this point you have some good, viable ideas. Part of your job now is to dig into these possibilities and further vet them against your Career Criteria. We want more than a bird's-eye view now. In this section, we'll refine your list, organize it, and hone in on your top ideas.

Refer back to your Career Criteria and grab your Top 3 Requirements (page 79). Go through your brainstorm in the previous section and eliminate any ideas or options that do not meet those criteria. Write the remainder of the list here. This should include all the roles that fit your criteria and get you excited.

Using this pared down list, do a little research on specific roles. Look up "a day in the life of (your idea)." Write down what you discover about those career paths here.

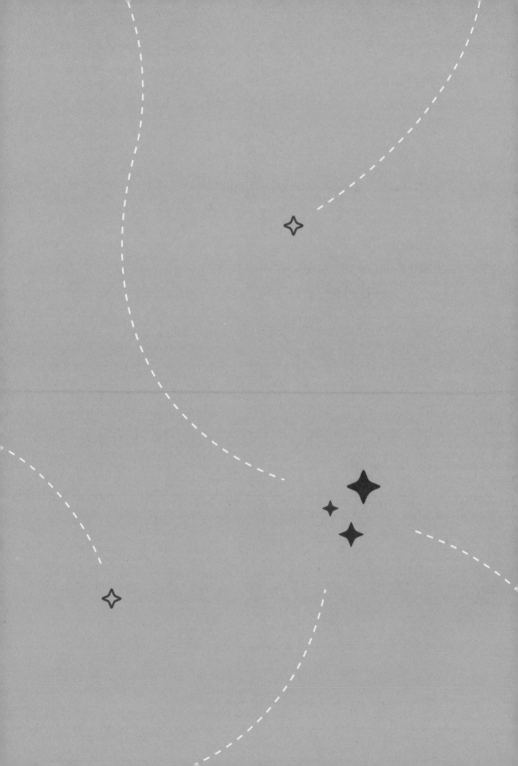

Search online for articles about the kinds of characteristics that contribute to success in the career path(s) you're interested in. Write them down here.

Explore online how you might pivot into the role(s) you're interested in. Do you need certain training, boot camps, or certifications? If you aren't sure, go to LinkedIn or another networking tool and search for people in those fields. What did they do to get to where they are today?

Set up informational interviews with people in the industry or at the company that aligns with your Career Criteria. Write down what you find out here.

Now that you've gathered information about potential paths and reconciled it with your Career Criteria list, you should have a sense of which paths are more viable than the others. Weigh them against each other and use this space to jot down notes about the conclusions you're coming to.

Creating an
Action Plan

At this point, you should have a path identified, whether that's a new role or a few companies you're excited about.

In this section, we will start to develop short- and long-term career plans. Short-term career plans include realistic goals and objectives that you can accomplish in the near future, whereas long-term career plans look at the bigger picture and include pipe dreams. (Pipe dreams are important too! While they may change periodically, they give you something to strive for along the way.)

The remainder of this journal will help you develop your strategic action plan for making these identified goals possible. Success comes when we identify a North Star and then clarify the concrete action steps we need to take to get there. This is where we build your thoughtful, strategic to-do list. Here are some ideas and prompts to get things going.

Take this space to write out your short- and long-term career goals as you see them now. A short-term goal should be achievable in the next 1 to 2 years, such as completing a certification course or breaking into a new industry; a long-term goal should be something you're working toward but is still 5, 10, or 15 years down the road, such as one day starting your own business.

SHORT-TERM GOALS:

....

....

....

....

....

....

....

....

....

....

....

....

....

....

....

....

....

....

LONG-TERM GOALS:

What do you need to do to meet these goals? One of the reasons we procrastinate in meeting our goals is because we haven't outlined the actual steps necessary to get there. Break each goal down into actionable, achievable steps and list them here; then add these steps to your weekly and monthly to-do lists.

Use this space to make a list of all the jobs, volunteer positions, and leadership roles you've held over the years, and the skills you developed at each. Perhaps you honed your presentation skills as a member of the debate team or practiced time management during your summer job at a newspaper. List those skills and experiences here.

Take the list of skills on the previous page and narrow it down to just a few bullet points for each role (and better still if they're applicable to the job you're currently gunning for). Make your abbreviated list of skills here, and then add it to your resume.

What keywords need to be in your resume and online profile so recruiters can find you and your profile will show up in searches? Look for keywords in job postings or online profiles (such as on LinkedIn) within your desired industry. Write those keywords here.

Go through your professional connections on social media, sorting them into different buckets based on how you might approach them. Think of this as mapping your network. You may want to ask some connections to go for lunch or coffee; with others, a phone call or an email might be more appropriate. (You may want to write a template email for reaching out to people.)

→ ☺

If you take people out to lunch or coffee, prepare ahead of time for this useful, one-time opportunity. Use the space here to write down the questions you want to ask them. What do you need to know that will help you connect the dots?

See if there are meetups, conferences, conventions, pitch nights, or other industry events you can attend. Even if you can't attend, there may be useful info on the event's website. You may find companies or thought leaders in the space you are interested in. Write what you learn here.

Are there classes, certifications, or boot camps that could help you pivot into your desired space, or make you a more competitive candidate for a specific role? Look for options at your local university, college, or community center. Try continuing education programs that offer video, online, and in-person courses. Use this space to take notes as you continue to learn about your desired industry, company, or role.

Are there relevant books, websites, newsletters, or podcasts you should check out? Perhaps there's a how-to book or an autobiography by a successful person in your industry. (This is a good question to ask in informational interviews!) These are all great ways to learn new concepts, trends, and lingo as you pivot into a new space. Do a bit of research and start a "resources list" here.

Brainstorm and collect the most common interview questions for the role and industry you're interested in through an online search. Write those questions and your responses to them here.

Go back to the question in the Career Personality section where you wrote about some of your big wins (page 38). Think about how you might tell those stories in an interview setting to convey your strengths and demonstrate how you deal with problems and overcome challenges. It's helpful to equip yourself with specific examples and stories before starting the interview process. Write your stories here.

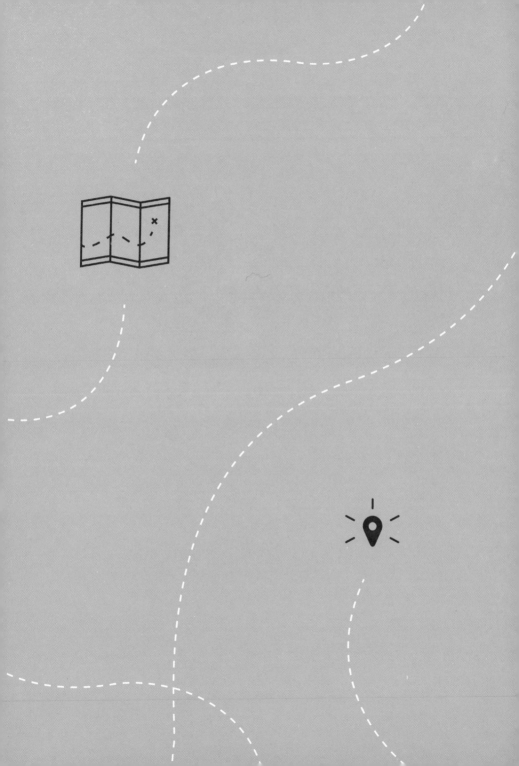

Are you prepared to negotiate? Learn as much as you can about the industry standard for salary and benefits beforehand so you're able to negotiate when an offer comes in. People who don't do this and simply accept the offer are potentially leaving thousands—even millions—of dollars on the table over the course of their career! Write your notes here: the package you're aiming for, the minimum you'd accept, and any other negotiation points.

Go back to the prompt where we went over questions to ask an interviewer (page 76). Now that you have a Career North Star, let's take another pass at this task. What do you want to know more about—the day-to-day tasks, the team you'd be joining, opportunity for advancement? There is a creative and appropriate way to ask these things of potential employers. Use this space to brainstorm.

You can use the remaining space in this journal to continue your research, make a to-do list, take notes during an informational interview, or map out a plan.

CONCLUSION

One of the biggest decisions impacting your quality of life is what career path you choose. Of course, you get to make this decision many times throughout your life, and you can change it whenever you like. How exciting is that?!

Think about it like this: You get to decide what your life looks like and how your career supports that. You get to decide what roles to interview for and what offer is acceptable. You get to decide when to work toward a promotion, when to pivot, and when it's time to quit. In sum, in your career, there are decisions around every corner, and you need to know what to base those decisions on.

The work you did in this journal gives you a basis for career decision-making on all levels. Save these materials so you always have them to refer back to. Many of the personality traits and interests you recorded here will remain constant throughout your career, so you can use this journal to make important decisions about your next career steps for years to come.

And because you picked up this journal and worked through this process, it's clear you are determined to make the very most of your work life and career, and the rest of your life as well. Kudos to you.

Now, onward and upward!

DR. COLLEEN CAMPBELL is the founder and CEO of Ignite Your Potential, a career, executive, and life coaching service. She has a PhD in clinical psychology and has been coaching clients in every industry, at all levels, for more than 12 years. She lives in San Francisco with her son, Daxton, whose name is written on her heart. Check out more of her work here: https://ignitepotential.com.